# CONFIDENCE
## MATTERS!

ZABED MOHAMMAD, PHD.
EDUCATOR & RESEARCHER
CANADA

EDITED BY
ROBERT HART

**Kids Edu Care**

Library of Congress Cataloging-in-Publication Data
ISBN: 978-1-998923-20-5

Publisher
Kids Edu Care Inc.
Children's Dedicated Learning Series
Website: www.kidseducare.ca
Illustration Copyright © 2023 by
Kids Edu Care Inc.
Canada


Illustration & Design
Bee Digital

🌐
beedigital.asia

✉
info@beedigital.asia

# WE ARE THE FUTURE OF THE FUTURE!
WE KNOW OUR STRENGTH. WE HAVE TO BE CONFIDENT, SELF-ASSURED, FOCUSED THINKERS WHERE WE CAN BELIEVE IN OWN ABILITY TO ENHANCE CAPACITY AND CAPABILITY FROM AN EARLY AGE.

## BUT, HOW?

WE BELIEVE,
IN A WORLD FULL OF ENDLESS POSSIBILITIES,

## "CONFIDENCE MATTERS"

IS A CAPTIVATING STORYBOOK DESIGNED
TO INSPIRE AND MOTIVATE TEENAGERS
ON THEIR JOURNEY TOWARDS A BRIGHT
AND SUCCESSFUL FUTURE.
THROUGH A COLLECTION OF ENGAGING STORIES,
THIS BOOK EXPLORES THE TRANSFORMATIVE
POWER OF CONFIDENCE AND SELF-BELIEF.

# JOIN US

AS WE EMBARK ON A SERIES OF ADVENTURES
THAT WILL ENCOURAGE TEENAGERS TO DISCOVER
THEIR PASSIONS, OVERCOME OBSTACLES,
AND EMBRACE THE LIMITLESS
POTENTIAL WITHIN THEMSELVES.

# THE SEED OF BELIEF!

AS TEENAGERS, WE HAVE TO REMOVE ANY
SHADOW OF SELF-DOUBT,
AND INSTEAD OF THAT WE HAVE TO EMBARKS
ON A QUEST TO UNCOVER THE SEED OF BELIEF WITHIN.
OUR TEENAGERS ENCOURAGED TO LEARNS
THE POWER OF POSITIVE SELF-TALK,
EMBRACING FAILURE AS A STEPPING STONE,
AND DISCOVERING THEIR UNIQUE TALENTS
AND STRENGTHS. THROUGH, THIS BOOK,
READERS DISCOVER THAT BELIEVING
IN ONESELF IS THE FIRST STEP TOWARDS
BUILDING LASTING CONFIDENCE.

# LOVE AND AFFECTION!

LOVE HAS AN UNMEASURABLE POWER
TO ATTRACT AND BUILDING HUMAN MIND
INTO A SELF- CONFIDENT INDIVIDUAL
WITH STRONG SELF-ESTEEM TO BE FORWARD...!

# PRAISE!

PRAISE IS AN ESSENTIAL ELEMENT THAT ALWAYS BOOSTS MINDS. AFTER EVERY ACTION WE EXPECT SOMETHING FROM OUR ELDERS, LIKE:

**WELL DONE!**
**GOOD JOB!**
**YOU DID IT!**
**I KNEW YOU COULD!**

# GREAT!
## WOW, AWESOME WORK!
## THAT'S INCREDIBLE!

**OR...**

IT'S OKAY, TRY AGAIN!
FAILING DOESN'T MEAN YOU LOSE;
IT BRINGS YOU CLOSER TO SUCCESS!
I BELIEVE THAT YOU CAN,
AND THAT WE ALL CAN!

# CHOICES!

MAKING CHOICES (IF THEY ARE NOT HARMFUL),
SHARING OPINIONS IS AN INDIVIDUAL
STRENGTH TO BUILD CONFIDENCE
AND ACHIEVE PARENTS' TRUST.
TO SUSTAINABLE THIS SENSE,
PARENTS ALSO CAN SHOW OR
EXPLAIN GOOD OR BAD EFFECTS
AND THEN LET THEM MAKE A CHOICE,
LIKE ABOUT WHAT CLOTHES TO WEAR OR WHAT FOOD TO
HAVE. CHOICES CAN ALSO INVOLVE PLAYING A GAME OR
READING A BOOK, ALLOWING THEM TO SELECT A PATH
FORWARD ...
TO SELECT THEIR VISION.

# SUPPORT AND MOTIVATION!

EVERY CHILD IS DIFFERENT,
ALTHOUGH EVERY CHILD HAS A SPECIAL
INTELLECT AND THEIR OWN INTERESTS.
BUT WHILE FROM CHILDHOOD ALL CHILDREN'S NEED
PARENTS' SUPPORT AND MOTIVATION TO FLOURISH,
FOR THEM TO UTILIZE THEIR TALENT IS AN
EXCELLENT WAY TO BOOST THEIR CONFIDENCE!

# POSITIVE ATTITUDES WORKS!

ATTITUDES ARE A PART OF GOOD MANNERS,
AND THEY HELP YOUNGSTERS TO LEARN AND
MANAGE POSITIVE BEHAVIOURS.
ALWAYS PROMOTING POSITIVE ATTITUDES
CAN INCREASE EVERYONE'S CONFIDENCE
AND ABILITIES IN A POSITIVE AND EFFECTIVE WAY.

BUT HOW?

WE CAN SHOW OUR OWN POSITIVE ATTITUDES
BY USING WORDS LIKE,

"I KNOW THAT YOU CAN DO THIS.
I BELIEVE IN YOUR STRENGTHS!
YOU CAN DO THIS!"

# RESPONSIBILITY AND ACCOUNTABILITY!

RESPONSIBILITY COMES FROM THE ACCOUNTABILITY.
NO MATTER, DO RIGHT OR WRONG,
WE HAVE TO APPRECIATE THEIR EFFORTS,
EVEN IF THE RESULTS ARE NOT PERFECT
THE FIRST TIME. SUCH GESTURES WILL
MAKE CHILDREN FEEL CONFIDENT AND HELP
THEM MOVE FORWARD WITH ACCOUNTABILITY.

# REALISTIC GOALS!

GOALS OR TARGETS
SHOULD BE REALISTIC,
AND BY FOCUSING ON THOSE GOALS
WE CAN SHOW THAT WE CARE ABOUT
THE RESULTS. ACHIEVING GOALS
WILL MAKE OUR TEENAGERS HAPPY
AND CONFIDENT,
SO WITH SUPPORT,
WE CAN SET AND ACHIEVE
BOTH SHORT-TERM AND
LONG-TERM GOALS. THIS WAY
WE CAN WATCH OUR CHILDREN'S
CONFIDENCE SOAR AS
THEIR GOALS
ARE ACHIEVED.

# CONNECTING WITH ADVENTURE!

GOALS CAN BE ORIENTED AROUND FUN,
SO IT'S A GOOD IDEA TO SET UP
ADVENTURE- OR PLEASURE-RELATED
ACTIONS THAT WHICH CAN ENCOURAGE
KIDS TO EXPLORE NEW HORIZONS.
FOR EXAMPLE,
BY ALLOWING
CHILDREN TO PLAY
IN PARKS AND FIELDS,
THEY CAN INCORPORATE
ADVENTURE  INTO
THEIR ACTIVITIES.

**LEARNING RULES!**

LEARNING STARTS AT HOME,
AND PARENTS ARE CONSIDERED THE FIRST
AND FOREMOST TEACHERS FOR THEIR KIDS.
SO, PARENTS CAN FOCUS ON SOME
DAY TO DAY PRINCIPLES AND RULES FOR THE HOUSE,
AND BY LEARNING THESE AS CHILDREN,
KIDS WILL BE SELF-ASSURED ABOUT
OPERATING WITH NEW RULES
AND VALUES IN THE FUTURE.

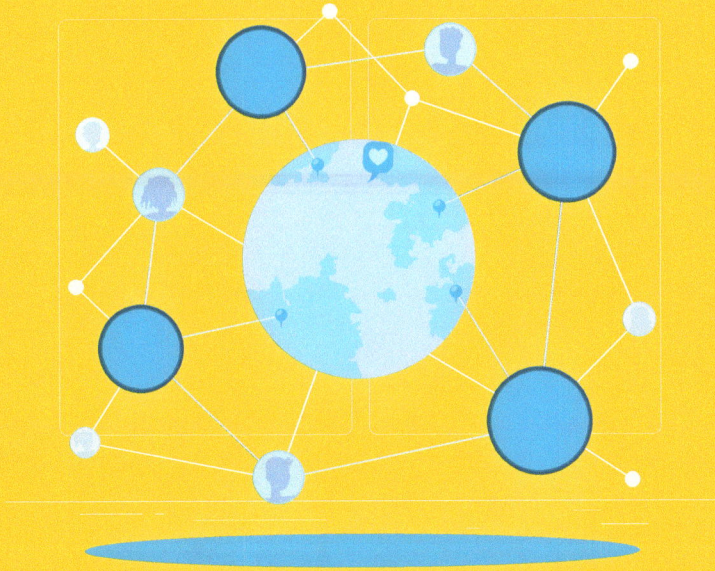

# INTERACTIONS AND

## SOCIAL CONNECTIONS!

TO ENHANCE CONNECTIONS WITH EACH OTHER
AND TO LEARN THE VALUES OF SOCIAL INTERACTION,
WE MUST CERTAINLY RELY ON OUR PARENTS
AND NEIGHBOURS.
THEY CAN HELP US TO LEARN AND EXPAND
OUR SOCIAL CONNECTIONS TO BOOST
OUR INTERACTION ABILITIES,
WHICH WILL HELP US ENGAGE IN
SOCIETY WITH CONFIDENCE.

# FACING CHALLENGES!

CHALLENGE HELPS US TO EXPLORE,
TO THINK-RETHINK,
AND TO CHOOSE THE BEST ALTERNATIVE.
WE OFTEN NEED THESE SKILLS,
AND SO IT IS ALWAYS GOOD TO
ALLOW CHILDREN TO FACE SOME
CHALLENGES AND SEE HOW THEY DO BEFORE
STEPPING IN TO HELP THEM.

EVEN WHEN WE DO STEP IN,
WE NEED TO BE GENTLE AND ENCOURAGE OUR KIDS
TO LEARN WHAT THE NECESSARY STEPS WERE.
ONLY THEN CAN THEY LEARN HOW TO BE READY
TO HANDLE CHALLENGES IN THE FUTURE.
ON THE OTHER HAND,
IF WE JUMP IN ALL THE TIME,
WE WILL RUIN OUR CHILDREN'S CONFIDENCE,
WHICH ONLY COMES WITH GETTING OUT
OF STICKY SITUATIONS WITHOUT ANY HELP.

# AVOIDING COMPARISONS!

COMPARISON IS ALWAYS GOOD IN
THE SENSE OF POSITIVITY. HOWEVER,
BY DOING THIS, SOMETIMES KIDS CAN LOSS
OTHERS CONFIDENCE AND ADOPT NEGATIVE ATTITUDES
WITH THEIR PARENTS AND OTHERS.
SO, WE NEED TO APPRECIATE THEIR
ABILITIES FOR WHAT THEY ARE,
AND INSPIRE THEM TO CONTINUE
TO PRACTICE SO THAT ONE DAY
THEY CAN FIND SUCCESS

# PROBLEM-SOLVING!

**PROBLEM-SOLVING REFERS
TO THE ABILITY TO SOLVE PROBLEMS EFFECTIVELY.
AS PARENTS, IT IS OUR PRIME DUTY TO
TEACH OUR CHILDREN HOW TO REACT
WHEN THEY FACE A PROBLEM,
AND HOW TO EFFECTIVELY APPROACH
PROBLEMS AND SOLVE THEM.**

# QUALITY TIME!

CHILDREN ALWAYS LOOKING FOR QUALITY TIME
WITH THEIR PARENTS, AND PARENTS NEED
TO DIVIDE THEIR TIME ACCORDING TO THEIR WORKLOAD.
AS CHILDREN LOOK TO STAY CLOSE WITH YOU,
TALK WITH THEM AND MAINTAIN A GOOD RELATIONSHIP,
LIKE SHARING INFO, AND ASKING QUESTIONS
AND LISTENING TO THEM.

# QUALITY TIME!

SHOW THEM THAT YOU VALUE
THEIR OPINIONS OR CONCERNS,
AND THIS WAY THEY WILL UNDERSTAND
THAT YOU CARE ABOUT THEM AS PEOPLE.

# BE A ROLE MODEL!

CHILDREN ADOPT
CHARACTERISTICS OF CHARACTER,
PATTERNS OF BEHAVIOUR,
ATTITUDES, AND PATTERNS
OF INTERACTION
WITH OTHERS FROM THEIR
PARENTS AND ELDERS.

# BE A ROLE MODEL!

IN THIS SITUATION, CHILDREN EXPECT THEIR PARENTS AND ELDERS TO SHOW CONFIDENCE, INDEPENDENCE, OPTIMISM, GOOD BEHAVIOR, AND MORALS AS EXAMPLES FOR THEIR OWN DEVELOPMENT.

AT THE SAME TIME,
THEY ALSO EXPECT THEIR PARENTS
TO APOLOGIZE WHEN THEY ARE WRONG.
SAYING SORRY SHOWS MATURITY,
AND WHEN WE ACCEPT OTHERS' FAULTS,
IT TEACHES THEM THAT THEY CAN
FEEL COMFORTABLE ABOUT TALKING TO US.

# CONFIDENCE!

CHILDREN NEED TO DEVELOP THEIR CONFIDENCE AS EARLY AS POSSIBLE, AND IT IS THE RESPONSIBILITY OF PARENTS AND ELDERS TO HELP KIDS OBTAIN SELF- ESTEEM THROUGH CARING AND GENTLE GUIDANCE.

STEP BY STEP,
WE CAN START ENCOURAGING DIFFERENT
TRAITS AND OBSERVE HOW OUR
BEHAVIOR AFFECTS THE DEVELOPMENT OF
OUR KIDS' ATTITUDES AND SOCIAL SKILLS.
AT THE SAME TIME,
WE CAN PROVIDE OPPORTUNITIES FOR THEM
TO DEMONSTRATE THEIR CONFIDENCE
AND COMPETENCE WHILE LOOKING
AFTER THEM ALONG THE WAY.

# EMBRACING INDIVIDUALITY!

IN A WORLD OBSESSED WITH CONFORMITY,
OUR TEENAGERS NEED TO BUILD
A SEA OF EXPECTATIONS. HOWEVER,
WHEN TEENAGER'S STUMBLES UPON
A GROUP OF EXTRAORDINARY MISFITS
TO CELEBRATE THEIR DIFFERENCES,
THEIR PERCEPTION CHANGES FOREVER.

# TOGETHER,

THEY EMBARK ON A TRANSFORMATIVE
ADVENTURE THAT CHALLENGES SOCIETAL NORMS,
ENCOURAGES SELF-EXPRESSION,
AND FOSTERS THE COURAGE TO BE AUTHENTIC.
THIS CHAPTER EMPHASIZES THE
IMPORTANCE OF EMBRACING INDIVIDUALITY
AND FINDING CONFIDENCE IN ONE'S TRUE IDENTITY.

# THE POWER OF
# UNITY AND COLLABORATION!

THE TWENTY-FIRST CENTURY
IS A CENTURY WHERE ALL ENCOURAGE PARTICIPATION
IN A COMPETITION; TEENAGERS WITH A PASSION
FOR ENTREPRENEURSHIP DISCOVER
THE TRANSFORMATIVE POWER OF COLLABORATION.
THROUGH A SERIES OF EXPERIENCES,
WE REALIZE THAT BUILDING
A PRODUCTIVE NETWORK AND WORKING
WITH LIKE-MINDED INDIVIDUALS
CAN LEAD TO TREMENDOUS SUCCESS
AND PERSONAL GROWTH.
THIS CHAPTER INSPIRES TEENAGERS
TO EMBRACE COLLABORATION,
BUILD MEANINGFUL CONNECTIONS,
AND LEVERAGE
## THE POWER OF TEAMWORK.

# EMBRACING RESILIENCE
# IN ADVERSITY!

IT MAY BE EVIDENT THAT SOMETIMES
WE FACE A CHALLENGING FAMILY SITUATION,
BUT WE FIND SOLACE AND PASSION AND RETURN
TO GOD.

THE UPS AND DOWNS OF THE JOURNEY
ARE A PART OF OUR LIFE. ALL TEENAGERS NEED TO
LEARN TO CHANNEL EMOTIONS INTO THEIR ARTWORK,
DISCOVERING STRENGTH AND RESILIENCE IN THE FACE
OF ADVERSITY. THIS CHAPTER EMPHASIZES THE
IMPORTANCE OF PERSEVERANCE, SELF-EXPRESSION,
AND USING CREATIVITY AS A MEANS
TO OVERCOME OBSTACLES.

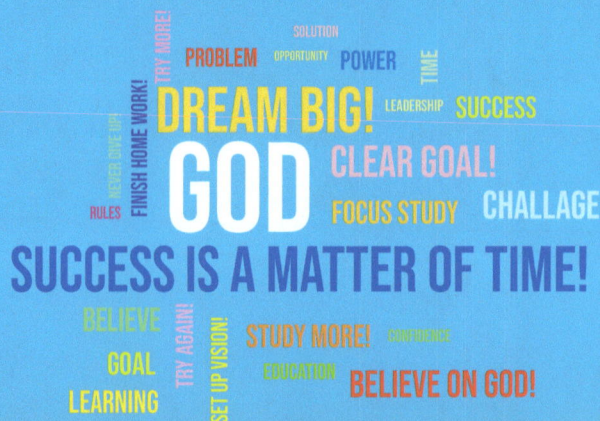

# FINAL REMARKS!

## "CONFIDENCE MATTERS"

IS MORE THAN JUST A STORYBOOK;
IT'S A SOURCE OF INSPIRATION AND MOTIVATION
FOR TEENAGERS ON THEIR JOURNEY TOWARD
SELF-DISCOVERY AND PERSONAL GROWTH.
THROUGH RELATABLE CHARACTERS,
ENGAGING NARRATIVES, AND VALUABLE LIFE LESSONS,
THIS BOOK ENCOURAGES TEENAGERS TO EMBRACE
THEIR UNIQUENESS, DEVELOP RESILIENCE, PURSUE
THEIR DREAMS, AND UPLIFT THOSE AROUND THEM.
WITH EACH TURN OF THE PAGE, TEENAGERS WILL BE
INSPIRED TO BELIEVE IN THEMSELVES,
DISCOVERING THAT CONFIDENCE
TRULY MATTERS.

www.ingramcontent.com/pod-product-compliance
Lightning Source LLC
LaVergne TN
LVHW072104070426

835508LV00003B/265